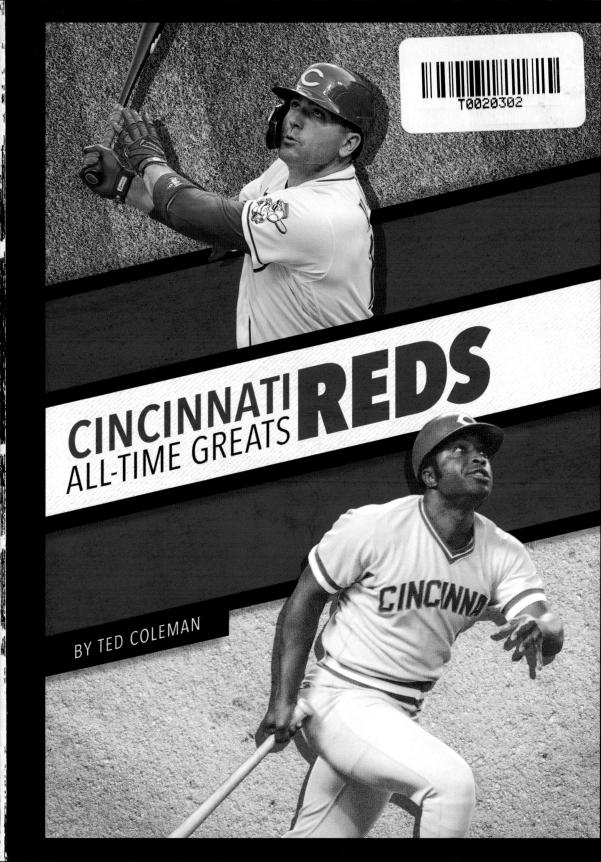

CINCINNATI REDS

ALL-TIME GREATS

BY TED COLEMAN

Book design by Jake Slavik
Cover design by Jake Slavik

Photographs ©: Aaron Doster/AP Images, cover (top), 1 (top); AP Images, cover (bottom), 1 (bottom), 9, 10, 12; Bain News Service/Library of Congress, 4, 6, 7; BH/AP Images, 14; Mark Duncan/PAP Images, 16; Tom DiPace/PACET/AP Images, 19; Jeff Dean/AP Images, 20

Press Box Books, an imprint of Press Room Editions.

ISBN
978-1-63494-503-5 (library bound)
978-1-63494-529-5 (paperback)
978-1-63494-579-0 (epub)
978-1-63494-555-4 (hosted ebook)

Library of Congress Control Number: 2022902486

Distributed by North Star Editions, Inc.
2297 Waters Drive
Mendota Heights, MN 55120
www.northstareditions.com

Printed in the United States of America
082022

ABOUT THE AUTHOR

Ted Coleman is a freelance sportswriter and children's book author who lives in Louisville, Kentucky, with his trusty Affenpinscher, Chloe.

TABLE OF CONTENTS

CHAPTER 1

THE EARLY REDS 5

CHAPTER 2

THE BIG RED MACHINE 11

CHAPTER 3

THE MODERN REDS 17

TIMELINE 22
TEAM FACTS 23
MORE INFORMATION 23
GLOSSARY 24
INDEX 24

GROH

CHAPTER 1
THE EARLY REDS

The Cincinnati Reds are one of the oldest teams in Major League Baseball (MLB). They joined the American Association in 1882. Back then, they were known as the Cincinnati Red Stockings. In their first eight years, they had seven winning records. Then in 1890, the team shortened its name to the Reds and left for the National League (NL). After that, wins didn't come as easily. Cincinnati didn't finish above third place for nearly 30 years.

In 1919, the Reds surprised everyone by making the World Series. Infielder **Heinie Groh** was one of the primary reasons why.

ROUSH

Groh was a skilled hitter and an even better fielder. He turned 333 double plays for Cincinnati.

Edd Roush led the team at the plate. The left-hander ended up winning two NL batting titles, one in 1917 and one in 1919.

The Reds' 1919 World Series win was controversial. Eight players on the other team, the Chicago White Sox, had cheated. Gamblers had paid those players to lose the World Series on purpose.

In the 1920s, the Reds went back to struggling. But Cincinnati did have a few stars.

LUQUE

THE FIRST PROFESSIONAL TEAM

In the early days of baseball, the players were amateurs. But some were paid secretly. That changed in 1869, when **Harry Wright** created the first fully professional team. The team was also called the Cincinnati Red Stockings. Wright's highest-paid player was his brother, George, who made $1,400 per season. The original Red Stockings lasted only two years.

Pitcher **Dolf Luque** was born in Cuba. He became the first Latino pitcher in MLB history. Luque led the NL with 27 wins and a 1.93 earned run average (ERA) in 1923.

In 1939, the Reds made it back to the World Series. They

got swept that time. But the Reds had enough talent to return to the World Series the next season. Pitcher **Bucky Walters** pitched 87 complete games from 1939 to 1941. He won 68 games in that stretch. He also went 2–0 in the 1940 World Series against the Detroit Tigers. The Reds won the series in seven games.

After that, the Reds struggled for two more decades. When they reached the World Series again in 1961, an all-time great was leading the way. **Frank Robinson** had joined the team in 1956 and was Rookie of the Year. In 1961, he

STAT SPOTLIGHT

CAREER SHUTOUTS
REDS TEAM RECORD
Bucky Walters: 32

ROBINSON
20

earned NL Most Valuable Player (MVP) honors.

Pitchers feared Robinson at the plate, and

fielders feared him on the bases.

CHAPTER 2
THE BIG RED MACHINE

In 1970, the Cincinnati Reds were back in the World Series. But they lost in five games to the Baltimore Orioles. One of Baltimore's best players was Frank Robinson. The Reds had traded the Hall of Famer to Baltimore a few years earlier.

However, the Reds had a new generation of stars. They formed one of the best teams in MLB history. **Pete Rose** earned the nickname "Charlie Hustle" for his intense style of play. He spent 19 seasons with the Reds. Rose retired in 1986 with an MLB record 4,256 hits.

Catcher **Johnny Bench** was an all-time great at his position. The two-time MVP retired in 1983. By then, he'd cranked out 327 career home runs as a catcher. At the time, that was the most of any catcher in MLB history. Bench's leadership guided the Reds to back-to-back World Series titles in 1975 and 1976.

The Reds of the 1970s also featured a deep pitching staff. Injuries limited left-hander **Don**

Gullett. He spent only seven seasons with the Reds. But in that time, he played in four World Series and won two.

Manager Sparky Anderson liked to use his bullpen. And he used **Pedro Borbón** more than anyone. Borbón took the mound in more games than any other pitcher in team history.

In the outfield, the Reds had slugger **George Foster**. Foster's career got off to a slow start. But in 1975, he became a star. Over the next five years, Foster led the NL in runs batted in (RBI) three times. He also led the league in home runs twice.

STAT SPOTLIGHT

MOST HOME RUNS IN A SEASON
REDS TEAM RECORD

George Foster: 52 (1977)

What truly made "the Big Red Machine" go was the team's talented infield. First baseman **Tony Pérez** swung for the fences. The seven-time All-Star hit three home runs in the 1975 World Series. Cincinnati defeated the Boston Red Sox in seven games.

Second baseman **Joe Morgan** earned NL MVP honors in 1975 and 1976. The Hall of Famer paired power with a mastery of reaching base. His career on-base percentage (OBP) of .392 is among the highest in MLB history.

Shortstop **Dave Concepción** partnered with Morgan for double plays. Not only did he play for the Reds for 19 years, but he played all winter, too. Concepción had grown up in Venezuela. He often went home to play in professional leagues during the MLB offseason.

SPARKY

The Reds of the 1970s had one of baseball's best-ever managers. Few people knew who Sparky Anderson was when he took the job in 1969. But he silenced critics by reaching the World Series in his first season. Anderson's players loved playing for him. He won two World Series with the Reds. He won another with the Detroit Tigers in 1984.

DAVIS
44

CHAPTER 3
THE MODERN REDS

After their 1970s glory, the Cincinnati Reds sank back down in the standings. They missed the postseason every year of the 1980s. Then they surprised everyone in 1990. That year, the Reds found themselves back in the World Series. This time they faced the heavily favored Oakland Athletics. No one gave the Reds much of a chance against the defending champions.

The Reds pulled off a huge upset. Outfielder **Eric Davis** had blasted 24 home runs that season. His two-run homer in the first inning of

Game 1 started off a 7–0 victory. The Reds went on to sweep the series for their fifth title.

Third baseman **Chris Sabo** also had a big World Series in 1990. The former NL Rookie of the Year racked up nine hits in 16 at-bats. He also hit two home runs in Game 3.

Shortstop **Barry Larkin** was the rock of the Reds for nearly 20 years. The team drafted the Cincinnati native out of college in 1985. Larkin joined the Reds the next year. He played his whole career for his hometown team and

THE NASTY BOYS

One of the biggest reasons the Reds shocked the baseball world in 1990 was their bullpen. Relievers Randy Myers, Norm Charlton, and Rob Dibble combined for 351 strikeouts during the year. They also helped the Reds shut down Oakland's powerful lineup in the World Series. Along the way, they became known as "the Nasty Boys." The nickname came from a popular Janet Jackson song.

LARKIN
11

retired after the 2004 season. Only Pete Rose
had more hits in a Reds uniform. Larkin was
also the NL MVP in 1995.

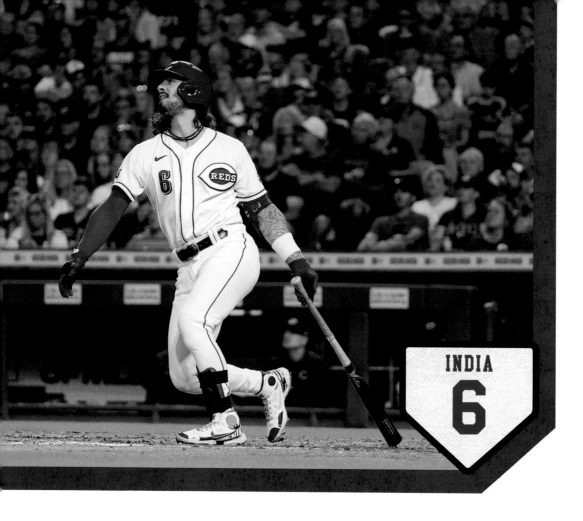

INDIA
6

The Reds struggled during the 2000s, but they still had first baseman **Sean Casey**. He hit with the best of them. Casey's friendly nature also earned him the nickname "the Mayor." He regularly chatted with opposing players who reached first base.

Joey Votto took over first base in 2008. The Canadian immediately became Cincinnati's best player. Through the 2021 season, Votto had a career OBP of .416, which was the highest in team history. He helped Cincinnati reach the postseason four times between 2010 and 2020.

Eugenio Suárez joined the team in 2015. By 2018, he'd earned a spot on the All-Star team. Suárez hit 34 home runs that season. Suárez wasn't done, though. The next year, he blasted 49. That was the most by a Reds player since 1977.

Second baseman **Jonathan India** put together a strong first year in 2021. In fact, he was named that season's NL Rookie of the Year. Reds fans hoped this young group of players could take the team back to the World Series.

TIMELINE

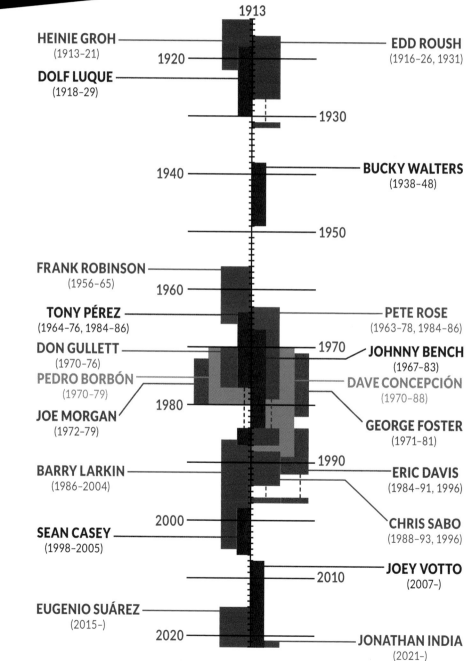

HEINIE GROH
(1913–21)

DOLF LUQUE
(1918–29)

EDD ROUSH
(1916–26, 1931)

BUCKY WALTERS
(1938–48)

FRANK ROBINSON
(1956–65)

TONY PÉREZ
(1964–76, 1984–86)

PETE ROSE
(1963–78, 1984–86)

DON GULLETT
(1970–76)

JOHNNY BENCH
(1967–83)

PEDRO BORBÓN
(1970–79)

DAVE CONCEPCIÓN
(1970–88)

JOE MORGAN
(1972–79)

GEORGE FOSTER
(1971–81)

BARRY LARKIN
(1986–2004)

ERIC DAVIS
(1984–91, 1996)

CHRIS SABO
(1988–93, 1996)

SEAN CASEY
(1998–2005)

JOEY VOTTO
(2007–)

EUGENIO SUÁREZ
(2015–)

JONATHAN INDIA
(2021–)

1913
1920
1930
1940
1950
1960
1970
1980
1990
2000
2010
2020

CINCINNATI REDS

Team history: Cincinnati Red Stockings (1882–1889), Cincinnati Reds (1890–1952), Cincinnati Redlegs (1953–1958), Cincinnati Reds (1959–)

World Series titles: 5 (1919, 1940, 1975, 1976, 1990)*

Key managers:

Bill McKechnie (1938–46)

744-631-11 (.541), 1 World Series title

Sparky Anderson (1970–78)

863-586-1 (.596), 2 World Series titles

Lou Piniella (1990–92)

255-231 (.525), 1 World Series title

MORE INFORMATION

To learn more about the Cincinnati Reds, go to **pressboxbooks.com/AllAccess**.

These links are routinely monitored and updated to provide the most current information available.

*through 2021

GLOSSARY

bullpen
A team's relief pitchers.

double play
A play during which the fielding team records two outs.

earned run average
A measure of how many runs a pitcher gives up per nine innings.

generation
A group of people who are all born around the same time.

on-base percentage
A measure of how often a player reaches base safely.

rookie
A professional athlete in his or her first year of competition.

runs batted in
A statistic that tracks the number of runs that score as the result of a batter's action.

upset
An unexpected victory by a supposedly weaker team or player.

INDEX

Anderson, Sparky, 13, 15

Bench, Johnny, 12
Borbón, Pedro, 13

Casey, Sean, 20
Charlton, Norm, 18
Concepción, Dave, 15

Davis, Eric, 17
Dibble, Rob, 18

Foster, George, 13

Groh, Heinie, 5–6
Gullett, Don, 12–13

India, Jonathan, 21

Larkin, Barry, 18–19
Luque, Dolf, 7

Morgan, Joe, 15
Myers, Randy, 18

Pérez, Tony, 14

Robinson, Frank, 8–9, 11
Rose, Pete, 11, 19
Roush, Edd, 6

Sabo, Chris, 18
Suárez, Eugenio, 21

Votto, Joey, 21

Walters, Bucky, 8
Wright, Harry, 7